THE CAULDRON

CHRISTINE BORLAND   ANGELA BULLOCH   DINOS & JAKE CHAPMAN

STEVEN PIPPIN   GEORGINA STARR   GILLIAN WEARING

FOREWORD

WHEN the Henry Moore Studio opened, in late October 1989, our idea was to offer a unique opportunity to major artists from around the world who would be invited to make use of the Studio in whatever way seemed most appropriate and necessary to them at that moment in their career. The Henry Moore Sculpture Trust would contribute practical and financial support of

 whatever nature and to whatever extent had been agreed. Our belief was that artists in mid to late career would benefit from an opportunity to step outside the pressure of their routine to make a large-scale project, take a risk or try a new direction – or simply, take a break for reflection and self-renewal. Our concept of a *studio* was not limited to a physical entity, but extended to include the metal workshops, foundries and quarries in the region. Indeed, anything or anywhere that was necessary to the production of the chosen work.

With nearly eight years experience of working in this way, we felt that the time was ripe to vary the rhythm. We chose to work with younger British artists, but to invite them as individuals selected for the strength of their past work and our conviction that they would continue to make interesting work in the future. It was at this stage, in 1993, that we turned to Maureen Paley for advice and I am grateful to her for the commitment that she has given to this project, which has required much time and effort over a period of years.

Although selected by Maureen Paley, the realisation of the project has been supervised by Chris Sacker whose role has been to assist the artists. In each case, the artists have chosen to make new work for exhibition in The Cauldron and to display their work in purpose built rooms within the Henry Moore Studio. When we converted the 19th century industrial spaces at Dean Clough for the making and display of new art, we avoided erasing the history of the place despite the inevitable inclusion of a number of white walls. Much of the work made for the studio since 1989 has connected in some way with the specific qualities of the

place, its fabric, history, technology and human significance. For The Cauldron, we have created a new space, sub-divided into individual rooms, purpose-made and freed of all history. This internal re-construction has itself taken on the role of a work within the project of The Cauldron, in a way that recalls the structures and spaces created by Aldo Rossi for the exhibition *Doubletake* at the Hayward Gallery in 1992. Our built spaces are rudimentary by comparison, but their significance is no less interesting because the transformation of the space at the Studio is more than just the making of white walled simulacra for the ideal white cube, it points to an attitude to space as *place,* which differs significantly from that of the majority of the artists, mostly of an earlier generation, who have worked with us at Dean Clough.

In his catalogue essay Gregor Muir describes the working process of each artist, their preferred environment and closeness to particular places and people. He describes a rootedness in *place* and provides a welcome corrective to the popular interpretation of so much recent art as wilfully confrontational, coldly post-human, or preoccupied with the anonymous territory of cyberspace. As a fundamental step in the preparation of this essay, Gregor Muir visited each artist to photograph and discuss the work in progress. In so doing, he preserved a vital link with the  purpose of the Henry Moore Studio, as a place for the making and display of new work that would approximate to the artist's own studio – whatever, or wherever, that might be; I am grateful to him for contributing, as a writer, to the process of the Henry Moore Studio.

Finally, I wish to thank Beck's Beer, and in particular Anthony Fawcett, for the financial support to enable us to produce this publication. Now entering its eleventh year, the Beck's arts sponsorship programme has developed an unparalleled reputation for for its long-term commitment to the arts in Britain, enabling a broad spectrum of artists and performers to create new work.

Robert Hopper   Director, The Henry Moore Sculpture Trust

IN the summer of 1950, Hans Namuth took over 500 photographs of Jackson Pollock at work in his studio, making it possible for the complete outsider to share in the energy of his production. Thereafter, studio documentation came thick and fast as the Pop artists in particular embraced the celebrity medium. Memorable footage includes a young Robert Rauschenberg astride a ladder in the chapel of a former New York orphanage while Andy Warhol's East 47th Street 'Factory' became renowned for all-night filming sessions which turned into 24 hour parties. Perhaps the most targeted assault on the need for a studio came in the late sixties with the emergence of earthworks and land-art. Momentarily, Robert Smithson's workplace became the Hotel Palenque, a ramshackle guest house in Mexico, while Richard Long set off with back-pack up Kilimanjaro. But the studio remains a mainstay in the artist's make-up, even at a time when the need for one becomes increasingly less certain. Surrounded by space saving devices such as computers and video cameras, why should an artist require a studio when art can so easily be made elsewhere? So, what of young British artists working today? Invited to make a new work at the Henry Moore Studio in Halifax, the artists who feature in *The Cauldron* – Christine Borland, Angela Bulloch, Dinos and Jake Chapman, Steven Pippin, Georgina Starr and Gillian Wearing – refused. The reason being, they are engaged in highly specific ways of working.

All the artists featured in *The Cauldron* have, at one time or other, produced work outside the studio environment. In 1991, **Gillian Wearing** took to London's busy streets and embarked on a series of photographs descriptively entitled *Signs that say what you want them to say and not signs that say what someone else wants you to say.* Confronted by the artist, members of the public were asked to write down on a sheet of paper exactly what was on their mind. The peculiarity of each statement, displayed by its author, compiles an absorbing account

of day dreams, anxieties, personal beliefs and aspirations. One photograph shows an elderly woman holding out a sign which reads, 'I really love Regents Park', while an unshaven student opts for 'Everything is connected in life, the point is to know it and understand it'. Snapped

throughout the early nineties, the series captured a nation in economic decline, measured by signs such as 'Will England get through the recession' and another, gingerly disclosed by a smartly dressed company employee, which reads 'I'm desperate'. The images of London's homeless are particularly jarring. 'Give people homes, there is plenty of empty ones OK!'

The sign continues, 'I have been certified as mildly insane', and ends with a touching plea, 'Come back Mary, love you'. Glancing through Wearing's photographs, the compulsion is to marry each person's appearance with their sign, back and forth, until the image reveals itself as an attempt to enter the invisible realm of other people's minds. Where we would ordinarily guess what people in the street are thinking, Wearing's signs endeavor to 'out' intangible thoughts and emotions – a form of impatience caused by not knowing what it is like to be in somebody else's shoes.

In recent years, single screen videoworks and video installations superseded Wearing's photographic output which included the 'sign' series. Initially, the bridgework from one medium to another was imperceptible as Wearing continued to ask Londoners to perform a task within a predetermined framework. Yet again, a broad section of the general public forms the basis of *Confess all on video. Don't worry you will be in disguise. Intrigued? Call Gillian...* (1994). The wording of the title refers to an advert placed in Time Out magazine which invited people to come forward and confess their innermost secrets. As promised, those who took up the offer are heavily disguised in a variety of wigs and masks, which number amongst them Ronald Reagan and Neil Kinnock. One after the other, a man confesses to sleeping with a prostitute, another to being gay and making obscene phone calls, and a woman who, having discovered her boyfriend was having an affair, drugged him, stole his credit cards and left him naked in a hotel room. An intriguing confession comes from a man unable to forget – his own words are 'file away' – the experience in his youth of watching his brother 'snog' his two sisters. As with the 'sign' series, Wearing's adherence to a preconceived framework ensures that the early videoworks are as unpredictable as the people they contain. More recently, however, Wearing's line of enquiry has focused on a more concise portrayal of the characters she encounters in everyday life.

Wearing lives on Camberwell New Road, South London, an area constantly referred to in her work. For example, *Dancing in Peckham* (1994) – a video of the artist head-banging to memorised music – was filmed in a local shopping mall, while the videowork *Homage to the woman with the bandaged face who I saw yesterday down Walworth Road* (1995) refers to the busy high street which links Camberwell Green to Elephant and Castle. Disguised behind a mask of bandages, Wearing's facial garb in *Homage...* is inspired by two people who left a lasting impression on the artist. The first, a girl believed to be on her way to a night-club in London's West End, the second, an Afro-Caribbean woman – often seen in the Walworth Road – who persistently paints her face white due to a rare form of psychological affliction. Further evidence of Wearing's streetwise inspiration occurs in *Western Security* (1995); a video and sound installation exhibited at London's Hayward Gallery which features a mock shoot-out between a bunch of rampaging cowboys. Largely inspired by her observation of the men who parade about Camberwell dressed as Clint Eastwood, *Western Security* acknowledges the South London area which, in Wearing's eyes, operates as a form of studio.

Wearing's preoccupation with the video medium brought her into contact with Kathleen Kenny and David Dawson whose company KD Digital is based in a Victorian terraced house in Kentish Town, North London. Wearing edits her videos in a room at the back of the house where a poodle named Boo Boo is commonly found asleep on the sofa opposite a gas fire. The all important computer, an Apple Quadra 840 AV, and two monitors are tucked away in a corner. Once a back seat driver when it came to 'non-linear' editing, Wearing acquired her computer skills by observing the process over a period of months. Initially attracted to KD Digital in May 1995, Wearing has practically moved in and describes this as her second home. Next to South London, it also serves as her second studio. Recently, Wearing has been working on a video triptych entitled *The Unholy Three* (1996); a fly on the wall glimpse at the private lives of a real life South London cowboy nick-named Young Guns, an acute caffeine addict who literally drinks tea in buckets, and glamour girl Claire who performs a series of risqué manoeuvres with an inflatable champagne bottle. All three eventually meet on a blind date in a Camberwell pub where the two men find themselves at loggerheads over Claire who is not in the least bit interested in either of them. Seemingly, when asked, most Londoners will do anything for Wearing whether it be confess all, or say what they want with signs. *The Unholy Three*, however, represents a subtle departure as Wearing continues to choreograph members of

the public, only this time within the confines of loosely scripted film. While the parameters of the early work were set by pen and paper, camera and confession, the present framework – into which people are placed and asked to perform – suggests a shift from understated to direct intervention. The space to watch, so to speak, is the journey from what other people might *want* to say, to how Wearing instructs them to perform.

While Wearing works in studious silence using a computer, **Dinos and Jake Chapman** can be found, most days, in their East End studio at the southern end of Brick Lane. Home to the largest Asian community in London, the surrounding streets are lined with Tandoori restaurants, wholesale clothes suppliers and ornate stores selling all manner of goods from Saris to sweetmeats, joss sticks to the latest Indian blockbuster movie. Since the late-sixties, a

number of artists have gravitated to this part of town. The most prominent being Gilbert & George who live in nearby Fournier Street where the suited duo are often sighted going about their daily business. Aside from working nearby, the Chapmans are related to Gilbert & George in as much as they worked as their part-time assistants throughout the late-eighties and early-nineties. With this in mind, there is always a temptation to link the two parties as both produce artworks that, in the eyes of the public, are deemed reprehensible. While Gilbert & George were once quoted as saying that their work was intended to 'un-shock' people,[1] the Chapmans continue to unnerve their audience with works such as *Zygotic acceleration, biogenetic, de-Sublimated libidinal model (enlarged x 1000)* (1995) – a circular clump of naked child-mannequins festooned with penises and vaginas. But any comparison with the work of their former employers begins and ends by addressing the possibilities of public indignation. Furthermore, Dinos and Jake Chapman rarely wear suits.

Viewed from across the street, the Chapmans' studio is an unimaginative blockhouse with a nondescript facade. Formerly an electrical sub-station, the building is presently occupied by a small contingent of painters and photographers. Sunlight rarely penetrates this part of the town and the gloomy corridors conceal all manner of obstacles at shin height. Ascending the stairs, the air becomes increasingly thick with the smell of solvents, spray paints, plaster and fibreglass. The Chapmans occupy three rooms on the top floor where they are often

found, pliers in hand, ripping the heads off mannequins. The first room – a hive of activity – is strewn with fibreglass body parts about to be reconfigured as Siamese twins with surreal genital deformities. Assisted by close friends Russell Haswell and Michael O'Mara, the Chapman team – a motley crew of young men who, as a form of occupational therapy, draw felt-tip obscenities on the wall – sport lowered face masks and overalls. Once glued together and sanded down, the child mannequins are skillfully air brushed, cosmetically enhanced and left to dry in an adjacent room. Illuminated by strip lights, the bald Siamese twins – wigs to be attached later – exude an eerie, haunting presence. Next-door, by far the messiest room, a huge clay mound covered in squashed brains resides like a cartoon island surrounded by a sea of junk. The floor is strewn with plaster bags, newspaper, dried clay, discarded paint brushes and modelling tools. The rubble is so deep that unintentional bridle paths have emerged as a way of negotiating the room. Inevitably, anyone who visits the studio will leave covered in dirt.

From the Chapmans' Brick Lane studio, works such as *Mummy and Daddy Chapman* (1994) – a male and female mannequin with genital- and anus-like protrusions – are shipped to far away galleries where they will no doubt rattle someone's cage. Not surprisingly, the production of such provocative works has won them much disapproval in the national press. In an article entitled 'The Fine Art Of Being A New Fascist',[2] Julie Burchill sought to compare the Chapmans with Hitler: an irrational outcry, recently surpassed by Martin Maloney who, in

Flash Art magazine, compared the Chapmans with one-time teeny-bopper band Bros – the direct comparison being with the band's front men Matt and Luke Goss. Observing the Chapmans at work, it is hard to believe that their present endeavours are capable of causing such widespread upset. They are, after all, two young sculptors engaged in a traditional studio-based practice.

When asked how they perceive their studio, the Chapmans liken their workspace to a machine that requires constant attention and, in return, will make all the decisions for them. Taken a step further, perhaps the studio is to blame for the video *Bring Me The Head Of...* (1995) which features a severed mannequin-head with a penis nose. Utilised by hired porn stars as a ridiculous dildo, the head symbolises a bold future for figurative sculpture which, in the hands of the Chapmans, is as utterly hopeful as it is perplexing.

Towards the end of 1995, Glaswegian artist **Christine Borland** was invited to live and work at Kunst-Werke gallery in the Mitte district of East Berlin. To this day, the buildings are scarred by the aerial bombardment and street fighting associated with the later stages of the Second World War. When Borland first arrived in Berlin, she felt compelled to trace the bullet holes which pock-mark the old grey stone facades – an idea she later abandoned. However, her tell-tale enthusiasm for such a project is indicative of Borland's fascination with the city's decrepitude and its ruination which serves as a constant reminder of her work. To date,
Borland has had all manner of everyday objects shot. At first sight, *Shoes With 9mm Hole* (1992) appears to be a perfectly ordinary pair of leather shoes until we notice the holes where a bullet has passed clean through the toes. A year later, Borland ordered the Berlin police to open fire on several sheets of glass with weaponry commonly issued to NATO and Warsaw Pact forces. It is from these guns that the work takes it title; *9mm Sig Sauer P6, 9mm Heckler and Koch MP5A37, 7.62 Natokaliber Heckler and Koch G3* (1993). Shot to pieces, yet remaining intact, the damaged sheets of glass are exhibited upright in open wooden crates so that we may inspect the damage inflicted by firearms on materials other than our own flesh.

In 1994, Borland exhibited *From Life* at Glasgow's Tramway gallery. The main body of the installation is contained within a number of Portakabins commonly used on building sites. The first contains a table whose dimensions allude to those of a dissection table. Placed on top, a partially opened cardboard box contains a disassembled human skeleton neatly packed in polystyrene wafers. Purchased from an osteological suppliers, Borland was taken aback when asked whether she wanted to order 'plastic' or 'real' bones. The second Portakabin contains slide documentation of Borland's research into facial reconstruction. The tension mounts as we enter the last of four Portakabin's where we find a beautifully cast bronze head – the product of a team of osteologists and an anatomical sculptor who were presented with one of Borland's mail-order skulls. To create a facial likeness, the first task of the osteologist is to establish the biological identity of the individual determined by the size and shape of the pelvic bones. Should a foetal skull be able to pass through the aperture of the pelvic bones, then the subject is believed to be female. Exhibited on a plinth, the final reconstruction is accompanied by text

which reads, 'Female, Asian, 5ft 2in Tall, Age 25'. The emotional detachment of the small print hits a raw nerve; 'At least one advanced pregnancy'. Unavoidably, we baulk at such a clinical summation of the emotions associated with sex, love and childbirth. Furthermore, it is shocking to think that this *person*, whose children may still be alive, was sent through the post in a cardboard box. As the work of an artist, Borland's facial reconstruction compounds the loss of identity associated with human remains. Typifying her most recent work, the language of forensic science with all its emotional vacancy is hijacked and steered towards a more impassioned assessment of what it is to be human.

While at Kunst-Werke, Borland made little use of her designated studio. Instead, she chose to work exclusively in the gallery where she installed a number of glass shelves high up around the room. The original ceiling lights were retained and any missing light fittings were replaced with spares retrieved from basements across Berlin. Seemingly, individual human bones of various shapes and sizes were placed on the shelves, dusted off and then removed, leaving behind a negative impression of the bone's outline in dust. Due to their close proximity, the lights shine through the glass shelves and project an image of the bone directly onto the wall below. With reference to Borland's exhibition *From Life*, Charles Esche wrote 'the act of reclaiming an image from an anonymous skeleton will clearly have a specific resonance in the new German capital'.[3] More than a year later, Borland's skeletal shadows enforce the likelihood of such a resonance and visitors to *From Life (Berlin)* may make a connection, not necessarily imposed by the artist, with some of the stories emanating from building sites across the city. At the present time, Potsdamer Platz – the former hub of Berlin – is one of the biggest construction sites in Europe. Once the site of Hitler's headquarters, the whole area is swathed with mystery. Allegedly, important finds have been hushed up during construction work. In view of Borland's Kunst-Werke show which opened in January 1996, it is hardly surprising that she was told the following story. A friend of a friend was on his way to work when he noticed builders exhuming bones on a newly excavated site in the East. He continued to observe this over several days until he eventually plucked up the courage to ask what was going on. The builders told him that they were under strict instruction to bag up the bones and hand them over to the police, no questions asked. Later, he made a deal with one of the construction workers and swapped two bottles of vodka for a sack of bones. The story was relayed by a local artist who suggested that Borland might want to see the bones – an offer she later declined.

In recent months, **Angela Bulloch** leased a studio in London's East End but has yet to acclimatise to her new workspace. Instead, she continues to work from home in Rotherhithe, South London, an area brutally disfigured by post-war tower blocks. Brandram's Wharf, on the other hand, is a respectable block of flats managed by a housing co-operative. Tastefully refurbished with post-modern trimmings, the old brick building backs out onto the river and provides an outstanding view of the Thames. From the first floor window, it is possible to watch tug boats as they wash waves against the huge industrial barges parked directly below. The front room is furnished with a black sofa, book-lined shelves and an office table. Bulloch's art materials, as such, include a telephone and fax – the means of long-distance communication with gallery technicians who produce much of her work on-site. It is possible that Bulloch's move to a new studio will permit her more time with the work prior to its installation, but then again, her approach is rigorously predetermined. Put simply, an idea is formulated then executed with little or no deviation. Understandably, Bulloch cannot afford to  experiment with something as complex as a motion-activated wall drawing machine. When Bulloch is reminded that it is practically impossible for certain artists, say Dinos and Jake Chapman, to work without a studio, she replies: 'Yes, because they're sculptors'. So why – when Bulloch has produced so many object-based installations, lightworks and drawing machines – does she fail to see herself as a sculptor? Bulloch replies with upheld palms; 'Certain artists need a studio to make sculpture, whereas I make structure'.

Exhibited as wall texts, photocopies and/or street signs, Bulloch's *Rules Series* is an accumulation of regulatory lists which include those that govern, strippers, 8 Ball, The Houses of Parliament and Bungee Jumping. There are even rules for the *Rule Series* – size of edition, copyright, ownership, dimensions and colour scheme. Moreover, Bulloch's spherical light works perform a variety of systematic functions – random sequences, on/off, fading, different colours, different rates, in line and out of phase. Clearly, Bulloch is one for regulating her own art which, in turn, reflects the malaise of regulations encountered in everyday life. Much of Bulloch's inspiration comes from the urban landscape. For her contribution to the opening of a new conference centre in Leipzig, Bulloch reconstructed a British-designed zebra crossing across a

pedestrian walkway. As a reinterpretation of the spherical light works, Bulloch's crossing represents a strand of her work which has much in common with architecture – a fruitful area where rules and regulations are concerned. In 1995, the Public Arts Development Trust commissioned Bulloch to produce a work in response to the River Thames which centred on a redundant concrete pier opposite Bankside – the site of the new Tate Gallery. Initially, Bulloch set about renaming the pier by projecting the imaginary place name 'Panorama Island' along its side. Since then, Bulloch sought the help and advice of London-based architect Jonathan Caplan to officially rename the jetty as it appears on the ordnance survey map. But the project does not end there. At the present time, Bulloch and Caplan have pooled their resources and developed an architectural proposal which would see the pier transformed into a riverside plinth.

While Bulloch moves freely from one 'on-site' project to another, **Steven Pippin** continues to work in a house adjacent to Blackheath Road – a busy thoroughfare where juggernauts hurtle on their way from Central London to Greenwich, Dover and beyond. Although Pippin used to live here, the house boasts little in the way of domestic comforts and, in accordance with more industrial requirements, the floors are stripped bare. Upstairs, at one end of a long corridor, Pippin has converted two rooms into a darkroom and a workshop. The darkroom immediately recalls a scene from Michael Powell's 1960 film *Peeping Tom*. Even the equipment – the enlarger, developing trays and chemical containers – appear to date from that time; 1960 being the year of Pippin's

birth. Taught the rudiments of photography by his father, an amateur photographer who would convert the family bathroom into a darkroom, Pippin recalls; 'In order to load a developing tank with film, which required total darkness, I accompanied my father into my parents' bedroom and their double bed. Under the bedclothes I was taught the procedure of loading a spiral tank with film'.[4] From as early as 1983, Pippin began transforming all manner of everyday objects – such as a fridge, bath tub, wardrobe and lavatory – into operative cameras.[5] In 1985 Pippin embarked on the first of his *Laundromat Pictures* achieved by inserting photographic paper and a customised shutter unit inside a washing machine. After the paper was exposed, chemicals were added through the soap compartment and the print developed by setting the machine to

a warm wash cycle. Taken inside various launderettes, both here and in New York, the resulting images provide murky views of the banks of washing machines opposite. Alongside

household objects, Pippin has also converted entire buildings into cameras. First, the interior is blacked out, then a small hole is drilled to allow for a sufficient amount of light to create an obscura, an inverted projection of the outside world, on the interior back wall. The image is then captured using large sheets of photographic paper which are developed before being returned to the same location. Sites for such photographs include a house in Clerkenwell, the upper floor of the ICA and Gavin Brown Enterprise, New York.

As might be expected, Pippin's workshop is in a state of elaborate turmoil. The shelves are piled high with bits and bobs, nuts and bolts, valves and transistors. A multitude of electrical cables, wires and leads dangle from behind the door and a lathe resides in a corner of the room – a reminder that Pippin once worked for an engineering firm. A collection of circular monitors retrieved from old TV sets, lie face down on the floor. Everything is pushed to one side to make way for a work in progress which occupies the centre of the room. Presently, the work consists of little more than an aluminium steel bench that, for the time being, recalls an earlier work – *Flat Field* (1993) – where a similar table-like construction supports a cylindrical chamber which, in turn, holds a rotating TV monitor. With *Flat Field*, the image on the screen – relayed via a video transmitter – is a film of a rotating model globe which, due to the counter rotation of the monitor, appears static. Pippin's latest work revisits the basic principles of *Flat Field*, only this time the central chamber is intended to revolve in all directions. Accordingly, the path of the monitor will assimilate a satellite's orbit around the earth. Similarly, Pippin's *Time & Motion Study* (1995) again centres on a slowly rotating monitor which relays a film of a clock whose 'second' hand appears static. Pippin's circuitous efforts may seem futile; after all, why go to such lengths to construct a rotating device that carries an image which outwardly appears still. But then synchronicity lies at the heart of these artworks. In order to maintain absolute stasis, each revolution has to be perpetually precise. Compared to Pippin's earlier photographs which thrive on process and duration, Pippin's time machines appear to be the product of a quality watchmaker.

In 1994 **Georgina Starr** was invited to develop a new work in The Hague. Alone for weeks on end in unfamiliar surroundings, she decided to redecorate her mini-apartment with all manner of objects and things. The assembled clutter includes a variety of party outfits either hung from the wall or carefully laid out on a chair. Like a teenager's bedroom, countless photographs, scribbled notes and mementos cover every inch of available wall space. Reminiscent of a collage by Kurt Schwitters, a photograph of the room forms the basis of *The Nine Collections of the Seventh Museum* (1994) and reappears as a CD Rom, a series of itemised photographs and an edition of posters with a key chart inventory. The CD Rom is an exceptionally  intricate piece. Using a touch screen facility, an object can be singled out and enlarged as an isolated image accompanied by explanatory text. One of the photographs on the wall – a close-up of the palm of Starr's hand – is categorised as 'No. 122. Den Haag Dagmarkt' (supermarket). "I became totally depressed when I was in the Den Haag Dagmarkt. I burst into tears in the fruit and veg' section. Lionel Richie was playing which made matters worse. I wrote a song on my hand." Each item is filed and collated according to the nine collections – The Lahey Collection, The Seven Sorrows Collection, The Junior Collection, The Recollection Collection, The Portrait Collection, The Allegory of Happiness Collection, The Visit To A Small Planet Collection, The Costume Collection and The Storyteller Collection. Using the CD Rom, we can explore each collection and every object within a room decorated with memories.

At the present time, Starr lives and works in Hoxton Square – a leafy Shoreditch park bordered by a huddle of refurbished warehouses. When she first moved to the area, Starr immediately set about converting her vacated studio into the location for a single screen videowork entitled *The Party* (1995). Starr plays the fictitious character Liz Dean who, in the opening scene, becomes disillusioned when she attends a party and decides to throw her own. In the following scene she constructs a makeshift drinks bar out of hardboard and timber. Later, she prepares party snacks in anticipation of imaginary party people, then mingles with invisible guests whom she entertains with fancy cocktails prepared, in slow-motion, to the musical accompaniment of Jean-Michel Jarre's *Equinox*. Wearing a silver dress, the Liz Dean character dances away to her heart's content. Clearly, this is her idea of a fun party as she is the

only one present in the room. In many ways, Starr's transformation of her studio and self recalls the rainy day antics of children left alone with a dressing-up box. Peculiarly photogenic, the most minimal costume change lends Starr the appearance of someone completely different. A multitude of imagined personalities abound in *Hypnodreamdruff* (1996) which comprises video projections, TV monitors, sound recordings, the type of caravan associated with motoring holidays, a bed, tinsel wall hangings, and various arrangements of tables and chairs. A frenetic collage of visual information, *Hypnodreamdruff* is divided into several stage-like arenas which centre on an imaginary night-club called *The Hungry Brain*. Developed from the closing scene of a 40,000 word script written by Starr the previous year, *The Hungry Brain* was originally shot in 1995 as part of the group show *Wild Walls* [6] at the Stedelijk Museum in Amsterdam. As the camera pans around the tables and chairs, we encounter people engaged in intimate conversation and the evening culminates with Starr's performance as the fictitious chanteuse Elena. Reminiscent of the scene in David Lynch's *Blue Velvet* where Dean Stockwell sings into a flashlight, Elena sings about a schizophrenic with four personalities all called Mary. Inside the caravan, a video back projection on the rear window reveals the antics of Dave – played by a

male actor – who irons his underwear and watches Lionel Richie live on TV. After Dave's sing-a-long with Richie routine, he prepares a meal for two. Sadly, he eats alone. In another part of the gallery, a bedroom setting incorporates a video reconstruction of the pyjama party scene from *Grease* with Starr performing all the female leads. If it were possible to enter the flash points of Starr's imagination, then we may well experience a cosmology not entirely dissimilar to *Hypnodreamdruff* which, in part, serves, as a working model of a highly active memory bank.

Continually being redefined, Starr's work process has become increasingly elaborate. While works such as *Crying* (1993) – a video of the artist doing just that – depended on the artist turning a video camera on herself, *Hypnodreamdruff* required a film crew, actors, a script and a certain amount of audience participation on the opening night of the Stedelijk show. To some, this would suggest that Starr is heading towards full-scale film production. However, as a director, sticking to the script is not necessarily in Starr's interest as she needs to unearth *something* about someone which she can respond to. For instance, when she discovered that the

man who plays Dave in *Hypnodreamdruff* also performs at childrens' parties, his entire routine of balloon-tricks became incorporated in the video. Clearly, Starr's observations of real people remain central to the work. As early as 1992, Starr reworked microphone recordings of unsuspecting members of the public into sound installations, scripted dialogues and song lyrics. Since then, Starr's observations have become less dependent on total strangers and increasingly charged with autobiographical reference points. 'A lot of the characters that I'm playing are based on people I know: my mother, a friend of mine, my sister. So I'm still using other people in my work, but I become sort of a vehicle for them'.[7] In this sense, Starr's studio is other people.

Over a period of time, Georgina Starr's Hoxton Square studio has come to resemble the cluttered apartment which features in *The Nine Collections of the Seventh Museum*. However, while Starr often reviews video material in her front room, the bulk of the work continues to be made elsewhere. Likewise, Christine Borland and Angela Bulloch continue to produce work on-site which suggests a certain disregard for the distinction between studio and gallery. As the only participating artists who are studio-dependent, Dinos and Jake Chapman and Steven Pippin would find it impossible to work elsewhere. In many ways, the Chapmans need to be surrounded by the carnage of abandoned works and wrecked mannequins which form an integral part of their studio mechanism. Surrounded by supplies of valves and transistors, without which his work simply would not function, Pippin's studio has an air of meticulous patience, not unlike a library, resulting from years of intensive labour. Gillian Wearing, on the other hand, as likely a candidate for the Henry Moore Studio in Halifax as any, would need to make allowances from her metropolitan experience. What typifies the work in *The Cauldron* is the extent to which it is informed by the urban environment. Furthermore, how can these artists *not* look out of the window and be reminded of their work? Wearing, like Starr, sees the people down below as subject-matter, the Thames reminds Bulloch of *Panorama Island*, the Chapmans see wholesale clothes suppliers and the exact same mannequins they use on a daily basis, while Borland walks down a street in East Berlin and contemplates bullet holes. Even the close proximity of Pippin's studio to the geographical centre of Greenwich Mean-Time, appears to inform his recent work.[8] While the works contained within *The Cauldron* may appear alien in relation to the local area, the exhibition as a whole offers the people of Halifax the opportunity to gaze through the artist's studio window – wherever that studio may be.

Gregor Muir

CHRISTINE BORLAND

Artificial Wounds and Sores, 5 Bleeding (detail)   1995

Underpass (detail)   1995

From Life, Berlin (detail)   1996

9mm Beretta Pistol

Inside Pocket 1995

Inside Pocket (detail) 1995

2nd Class Male, 2nd Class Female (detail)   1996

2nd Class Male, 2nd Class Female (detail)   1996

ANGELA BULLOCH

Round Table with Mae West   1995

Panorama Island   1995

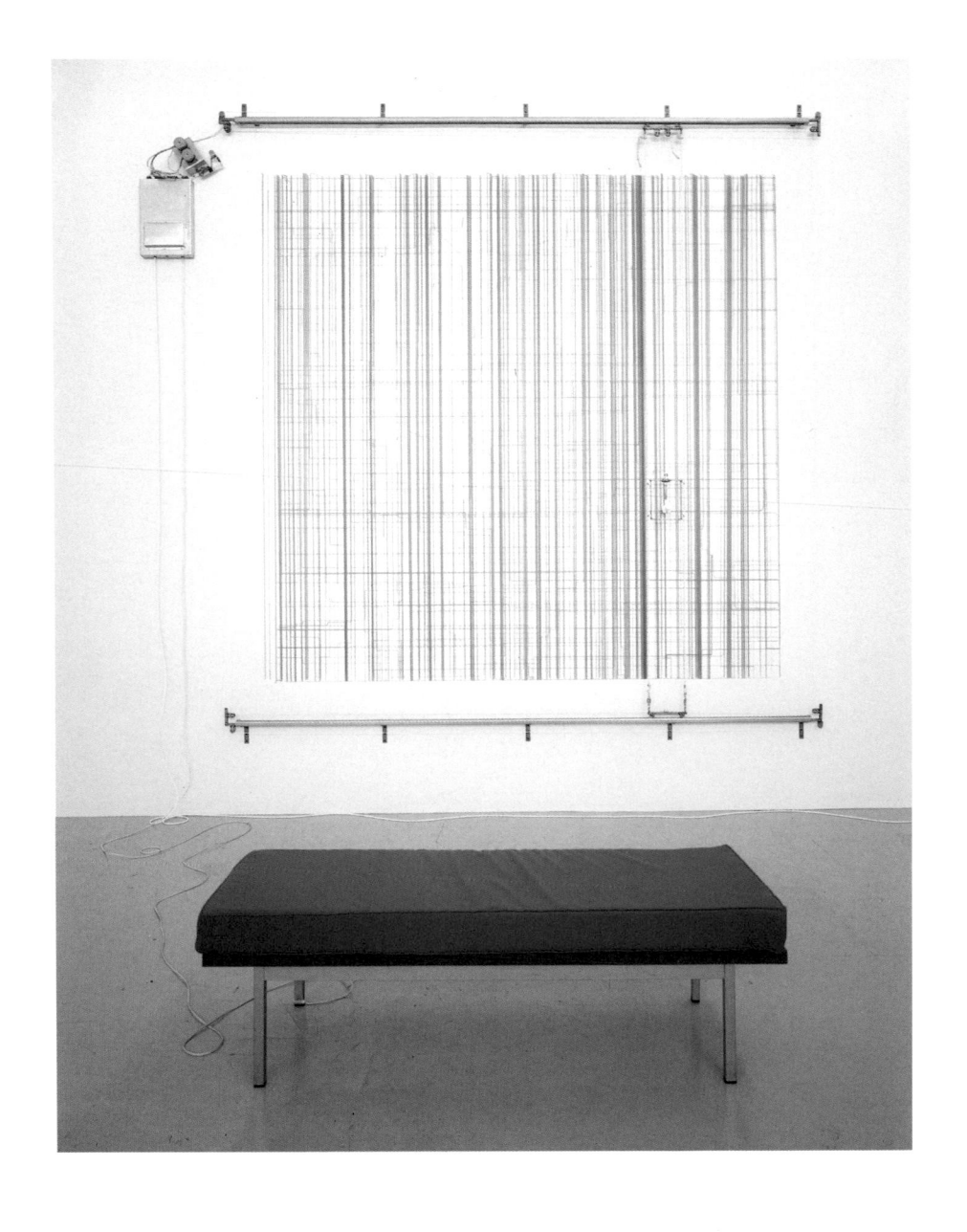

Betaville   1994

Betaville, Happy Sack with Notebooks, 8 Raptures with Remoconboy, Random Reminder   1995

Inside the image:

R360
1. Remove all items from your pockets.
2. Strap yourself firmly into the seat.
3. Put £3 in the slot and press start.
4. You are advised not to play the game if any of the following applies:

a) You are shorter than 130cm. b) You are intoxicated. c) You have heart problems.
d) You are pregnant. e) You have high or low blood pressure.
f) Your doctor has advised you to avoid strenuous exercise.
g) You have any mental or physical problems.

R360 1996

Grand Stand and the Marxist Myth (A Light Lowered, A Floor Raised, A Sound Bounced)   1996

Remocon Bags with Grand Stand   1994/1996

Great Deeds Against the Dead   1994

The graphic promise
We are sore-eyed scopophiliac oxymorons. Or, at least, we are disenfranchised aristocrats, under siege from our feudal heritage.
of our absent but nevertheless sonorous letraset, honours the dead (and the bad conscience) of past generations, a recollection of the discordance between
concepts and pictures. Our discourse offers a benevolent contingency of concepts, a discourse of end-of-sale remnants, a rationalistic hotbed of sober
categories. We have manufactured our products according to the market demands of a deconstructive imperitive, and policed them according to the rules of
an industrial dispute – our bread is buttered on both sides. We have always already been functions of a discourse; in short, our subjectivity (our labour)
deserves professional interpretation, our mental agitation demands a limitless expressionism, our contractual teleology demonstrates our servility to a cultural
climax never to be experienced. The future remains excluded. But sometimes, against the freedom of work, we phantasise emancipation from this liberal polity,
into a superheavyweight no-holds-barred all-in mud wrestling league, a scatological aesthetics for the tired of seeing.

We are Artists   1992

Zygotic acceleration, biogenetic, de-sublimated libidinal model (enlarged x 1000)   1995

Übermensch (detail)   1995

Gold, Silver & Shit   1996

Gold, Silver & Shit   1996

Negative Perspective 1995

Cosmos (detail)   1995

Stereophonic Wow & Flutter   1994

opposite

Horizontal Hold
1996

Sketch for **Horizontal Hold**
1996

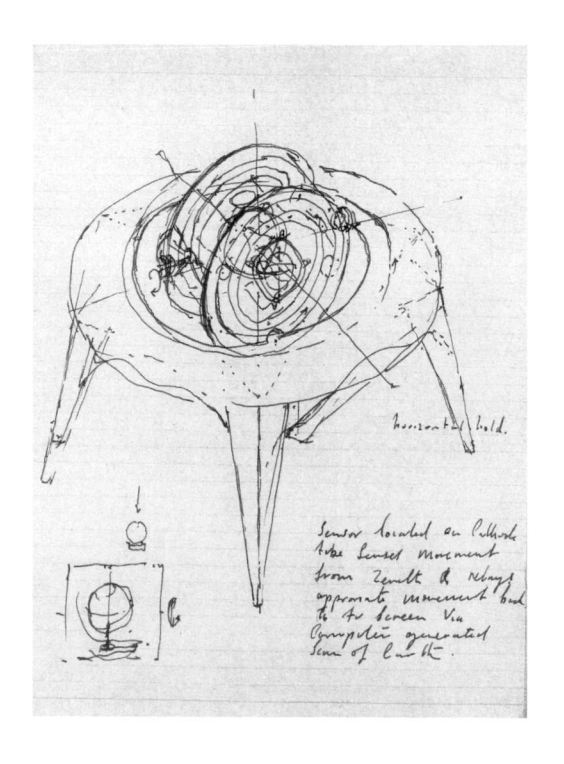

[41]   **Steven Pippin**

Horizontal Hold   1996

Horizontal Hold   1996

The Nine Collections of the Seventh Museum   1994

Crying 1993

The Party, Entertaining the Guests   1995

Hypnodreamdruff: The Hungry Brain, Elena singing Schizophrenia (detail)   1996

Drivin On   1996

Drivin On (detail) 1996

Dancing in Peckham   1994

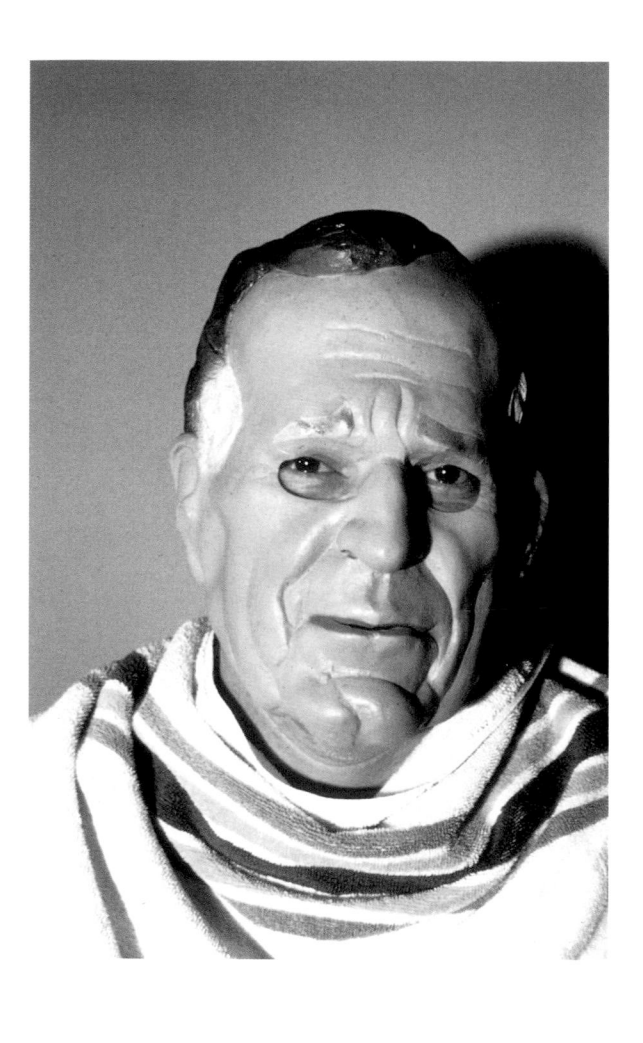 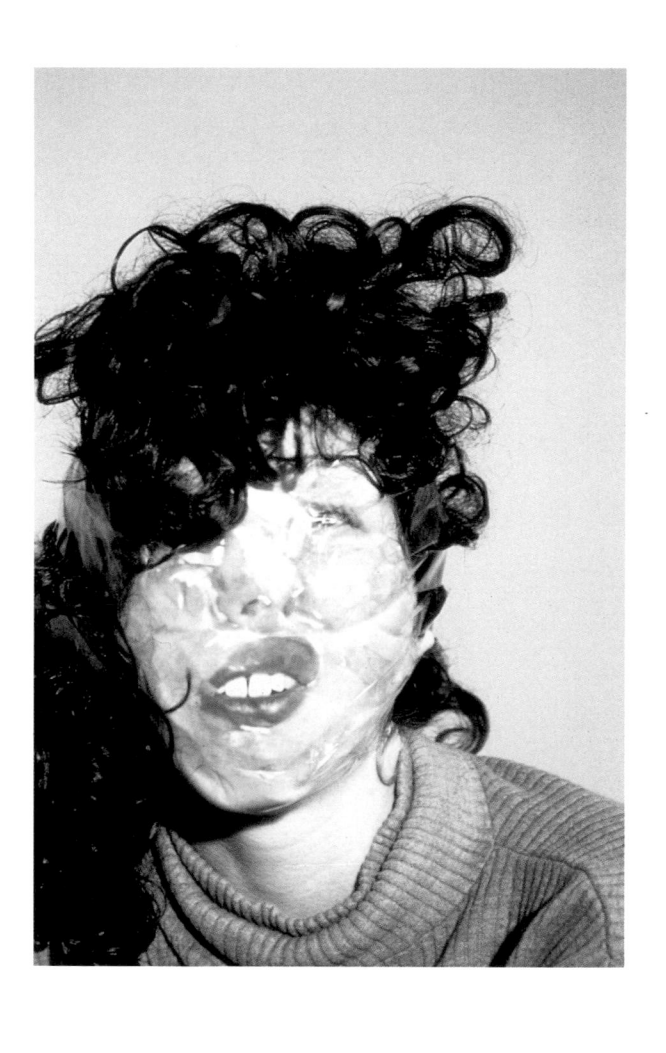

Confess all on video. Don't worry you will be in disguise. Intrigued? Call Gillian…   1994

Signs that say what you want them to say and not signs that say
what someone else wants you to say   1992–93

Homage to the woman with the bandaged face who I saw yesterday down Walworth Road 1995

60 Minutes Silence   1996

60 Minutes Silence 1996

Gillian Wearing

CHRISTINE BORLAND

born 1965, Darvel, Ayrshire

Education

1983–87 BA Hons, Glasgow School of Art
1987–88 MA, University of Ulster, Belfast

Solo Exhibitions

1994 From Life, Glasgow, Tramway, Glasgow ★
1995 Inside Pocket, The British Council
Gallery, Prague
1996 From Life, Berlin, Kunstwerke, Berlin ★
Galerie Eigen & Art, Leipzig
Sawn-Off, Gallery Enkehuset, Stockholm
One Person Exhibition, Frac Langudoc
Roussilon, Montpelier

Group Exhibitions

1991 Kunst Europa, Kustverein, Karlsruhe ★
Speed, Transmission Gallery, Glasgow
The Living Room Project, curated by
Giani Piacenti for his Living Room,
Glasgow
1992 Contact, Transmission Gallery, Glasgow
Guilt by Association, Irish Museum of
Modern Art, Dublin
In and Out/Back and Forth, 578
Broadway, New York ★
Artists Show, Artists Galerie Vier, Berlin
1993 Christine Borland & Craig Richardson,
Chisenhale Gallery, London
Underlay, Spring Street, Soho, New York
Aperto, Venice Biennale
Fontanelle, Kunstpeicher, Potsdam
2nd Tyne International, Newcastle
Wonderful Life, Lisson Gallery, London
Walter Benjamin's Briefcase, Moagens
Harmonia, Oporto
Left Luggage Rencontres dans un Couloir,
Hou Hanru, Paris and tour
1994 The Spine, De Appel Foundation,
Amsterdam ★
Watt, Witte de Witte Centre for
Contemporary Art and Kunsthal,
Rotterdam ★
The Gaze, Carré des Arts, Parc Florale de
Paris ★
Ik & De Ander, Dignity for All;
Reflections on Humanity, Beurs Van
Berlage, Amsterdam ★
East of Eden, Schloss Mosigkau, near
Dessau ★
Riviera, Oriel Mostyn, Llandudno ★

Little House on the Prairie, Marc Jancou
Gallery, London
Art Unlimited, Arts Council Collection
exhibition toured by National
Touring Exhibitions from the Hayward
Gallery ★
Institute of Cultural Anxiety, ICA,
London
Heart of Darkness, Kröller Müller
Museum, Otterlo
1995 Eigen & Art at IAS, Independent Art
Space, London
In Search of the Miraculous, (In honour of
Bas Jan Ader), Starkmann
Library Services, London
External Links, Mackintosh Museum,
Glasgow School of Art, Glasgow
Wild Roses Grow By The Roadside,
52c Brick Lane, London
SWARM, The Scottish Arts Council
Traveling Gallery
New Art in Britain, Museum Sztuki,
Lodz ★
Pulp Fact, The Photographers' Gallery,
London
Maikafer Flieg, The Shelter, Köln-
Ehrenfeld, Cologne
Breakfast in Budapest, Uljak Exhibition
Hall, Budapest
You Show, Galerie Hans Knoll, Budapest
The British Art Show 4, Manchester,
Cardiff and Edinburgh ★
1996 Christine Borland, Roddy Buchanan,
Jacqueline Donahie, Douglas Gordon,
Galerie Eigen & Art, Berlin
21 Days of Darkness, Transmission
Gallery, Glasgow
Hebben Wij Het Geweten, Provincial
Museum Voor Actuele Kunst, Hasselt,
Belgium
Nach Weimar, Neues Museum, Weimar
More Time, Less History, Fundacio de
Serralves, Oporto
The Cauldron, The Henry Moore Studio,
Dean Clough, Halifax ★

★ Denotes accompanying publication

ANGELA BULLOCH

born 1966, Ontario, Canada

Education

1985–88 BA Hons Fine Art, Goldsmith's College, University of London

Awards

1989   Whitechapel Artists Award
1994   Two months artist residency ARCUS-project MORIYA, Japan

Solo Exhibitions

1990   Interim Art, London
        APAC, Centre d'Art Contemporain, Nevers
        Galerie Claire Burrus, Paris
        Esther Schipper, Cologne
1991   Le Case d'Arte, Milan
1992   Esther Schipper, Cologne
        Galleria Locus Solus, Genova, Italy
1993   1301, Santa Monica, California
        the art of survival/baby-doll saloon, together with Sylvie Fleury at Laure Genillard Gallery, London
        Rules Series, Esther Schipper, Cologne
        Centre pour Création Contemporaine, Tours, France
1994   Frac Languedoc-Rousillons Aldebaran-Espace d'Art Contemporain Espace Vigneron, Baillargues; Kunstverein in Hamburg, Hamburg
1995   Mudslinger, Schipper & Krome, Cologne
        From the chink to Panorama Island, PADT London

Group Exhibitions

1988   Freeze, Part I, Docklands, London ★
        Freeze, Part III, Docklands, London
1989   Home Truths, six British artists, Castello di Rivara, Torino ★
        Bulloch, Hume, Landy, Esther Schipper, Cologne ★
1990   In Loving Correspondence, Massimo Audiello Gallery, New York
        Seven Obsessions, Whitechapel Art Gallery, London
        Common Market, Richard Kuhlenschmidt Gallery, Los Angeles
        The Köln Show, in nine Cologne galleries ★

1991   Reve, Fantaisie, Galerie du Mois, Paris
        Angela Bulloch, Sarah Seager and Craig Wood, Interim Art, London
        Victoria Miro Gallery, London
        no man's time, Villa Arson, Nice ★
        Projezioni, Castello di Rivara, Torino
        Broken English, Serpentine Gallery, London
        Plastic Fantastic Lover (object à), Blum Helman Warehouse, New York ★
        Devices, Josh Baer Gallery, New York
        Marking Time, The Drawing Center, New York
1992   Il faut construire l'hacienda, CCC Tours ★
        Etats Specifiques – 11 Artistes Anglais, Musée des Beaux-Arts
        André Malraux, Le Havre ★
        Lying on top of a building the clouds seemed no nearer than they had when I was lying on the street, Monika Sprüth Galerie, Cologne, Le Case D'Arte, Milan
        Dirty Data-Sammlung Schürmann, Ludwig Forum für Internationale Kunst, Aachen ★
        Still, Andrea Rosen Gallery, New York
        Angela Bulloch, Adam Chodzo..., instructions received by Liam Gillick, Gio Marconi, Milan
        Lily van der Stokker, Angela Bulloch, Stéphane Magnin (Wall Drawings), Air de Paris, Nice ★
        Informationsdienst, Traveling exhibition first presented in Ausstellungsraum Künstlerhaus Stuttgart, Germany
        Manifesto, Daniel Buchholz, Cologne; Castello di Rivara, Torino; Wacoal Arts Centre, Tokyo; Urbi et Orbi, Paris
        ON, with Henry Bond, Liam Gillick, Graham Gussin, Markus Hansen, Interim Art, London, until Feb. 1993 ★
        240 minute video compilation by Lothar Hempel and Georg Graw, Esther Schipper, Cologne
1993   Documentario 2, Spazio Opos, Milan ★
        Tutto Tondo, Monika Sprüth Gallery, Cologne
        Esther Schipper at the Christopher Grimes Gallery, Santa Monica
        Galerie Walcheturm, Zurich
        Aperto, Venice Biennale ★
        Summer 93, Air de Paris, Nice

Nulle Part et partout, Espace Paul Boyé
Sète, France
My Little Toilet, Glasgow
London Photo Race, Friesenwall 120,
Cologne
Christmas Shop, Air de Paris à Paris, Paris
Unplugged: the demo video tape,
The Holiday
Inn, Cologne (accompanying video
compilation)
Dokumentationsraum, Esther Schipper,
Cologne
Dancing Girls, (with Kate Daw) Store 5,
Melbourne
An old song and a new drink, (with Liam
Gillick) Café Beaubourg, Paris
Viennese Story, Viennese Secession,
Vienna

1994   Surface de Réparations, Espace Frac,
Dijon
blup/bleep, Westwerk e.V., Hamburg
The Antidote, Centre 181 Gallery, London
Cloni, 'The Box', A & M Bookstore, Milan
WM karaoke, (with Liam Gillick),
Portikus Frankfurt, Frankfurt, a.M
Brian Butler – 1301 (L.A.) presents :
Angela Bulloch, Meg Cranston, Sarah
Seager, Thaddeus Strode at the Guest
Room of Art & Public, Geneva
Surface de Réparations II, Espace Frac,
Dijon
The Institute of Cultural Anxiety, ICA,
London
Mixbild, Schipper & Krome, Cologne
Wall to Wall, Leeds City Art Gallery ★
temporary translation(s), Sammlung
Schürmann, Deichtorhallen Hamburg ★
Sammlung Schürmann in Suermont
Ludwig Museum, Aachen
Monaco Grand Prix 94, Galleries in Nice
and Monaco
New reality mix, Performance and video
weekend, Stockholm
Use your allusion, recent video art,
Museum of Contemporary Art, Chicago

1995   Wohnzimmer, Schipper & Krome,
Cologne
Toys, Nicolas Bourriaud & Eric Troncy
for Documents, Galerie Jousse Seguin
Corpus delicti, Kunstforeningen,
Copenhagen ★

Faction Video, Det Kongelige Danske
Kunstakademi, Copenhagen
Stoppage, CCC Tours
En Passant...Urban Scenes in
Contemporary Art, Akademie der
Bildenden Künste, Vienna ★
Das Ende der Avantgarde, Kunst als
Dienstleitung, Kunsthalle der
Hypo-kulturstiflung, Munich ★
444 & 222 Too, South London Gallery,
London
Sage, with Sam Taylor Wood, Gillian
Wearing, Elisabeth Wright
Galerie Michael Rein, Tours
Klangskulpturen, Augenmusik, Ludwick
Museum, Koblenz ★
La Labyrinthe Moral, Le Corsortium,
Dijon
Am Rande der Malerei, (second part),
Kunsthalle Bern, Bern ★
Space Odyssey, Eleni Koroncou Gallery,
Athens ★
How is everything, Vienese Secession,
Vienna

1996   Traffic, Musée d'art contemporain,
Bordeaux ★
The Cauldron, The Henry Moore Studio,
Dean Clough, Halifax ★

★ Denotes accompanying publication

DINOS & JAKE CHAPMAN

Dinos Chapman

born 1962

Education

1979–81 Ravensbourne College of Art (BA)
1988–90 Royal College of Art (MA)

Jake Chapman

born 1966

Education

1985–88 North East London Polytechnic
(BA Hons.)
1988–90 Royal College of Art (MA)

Dinos & Jake Chapman

Solo Exhibitions

1992 We Are Artists, Hales Gallery, London
1993 The Disasters of War, Victoria Miro
Gallery, London
1994 Mummy & Daddy, Galeria Franco Toselli,
Milan
Great Deeds Against the Dead, Victoria
Miro Gallery, London
1995 Five Easy Pissers, Andrehn-Schiptjenko,
Stockholm
Gavin Brown's enterprise, New York
Bring me the head of..., Ridinghouse
Editions, London
Zygotic acceleration, biogenetic, de-
sublimated libidinal model (enlarged x
1000), Victoria Miro Gallery, London
P–House, Tokyo, Japan
Chapmanworld, ICA, London *

Group Exhibitions

1993 Matter & Fact, Katherine Hamnett
Building, London *
1994 Watt, With de Witte & Kunsthal
Rotterdam *
Great Deeds Against the Dead, Andrea
Rosen, New York
Five British Artists, Andrehn Schiptjenko,
Stockholm
Rien à Signaler, Galerie Analix, Geneva *
Liar, Hoxton Square, London
1995 The Institute of Cultural Anxiety: Works
from the Collection, ICA, London *
London-Nu, Kunstforeningen,
Copenhagen *

General Release: Young British Artists,
Venice Biennale, Scuola di San Pasquale,
Venice *
Brilliant!: New Art from London, Walker
Art Center, Minneapolis *
1996 Brilliant!: New Art from London,
Museum of Contemporary Art, Houston
The Cauldron, The Henry Moore Studio,
Dean Clough, Halifax *

* Denotes accompanying publication

STEVEN PIPPIN

born 1960, Redhill

Education

1976–78 ONC in Mechanical Engineering, Charles Keene College, Leicester

1981–82 Foundation Course in Art & Design, Loughborough College, Leicestershire

1982–85 BA Fine Art Sculpture, Brighton Polytechnic

1986–87 MA Fine Art, Chelsea School of Art, London

Solo Exhibitions

1993 Introspective, ICA, London

1994 Migrateurs, ARC, Musée d'Art Moderne, Paris

Retrospective, A/C Projectroom/enterprise, New York

Interior, Regen Projects, Los Angeles

Omnigraph, Jack Hanley Gallery, San Francisco

Work from the Recession, Victoria Miro Gallery, London

Addendum, Portikus, Frankfurt am Main

1995 Time & Motion, FRAC Limousin, Limoges

Negative Perspective, Ujazdowskie Castle, Warsaw

Group Exhibitions

1986 New British Sculpture, Air Gallery, London

1987–88 Germinations IV London, Marseilles, Breda & Bonn

1990 Launderama, London Film Festival (Film Co-op), Leicester Film

Festival, & Kino Club, South London

1991 Artist in Residence at Sculpture Space, Utica, New York

1992 Insignificant, 10 East 39th St, Suite 525, New York

Twelve British Artists, Barbara Gladstone, New York

1993 Max Hetzler Gallery, Cologne

Aperto, Venice Biennale

Behind Closed Doors, Milan

Wonderful Life, Lisson Gallery, London

Chambre 763 Carlton Palace Hotel, Paris

Self Winding, Nanba City Hall, Osaka & Sphere Max, Tokyo

Projects 44, Museum of Modern Art, New York

1994 Cloaca Maxima, Museum der Stadtentwasserung, Zurich

Audience 0.01, Flash Art Museum, Trevi

Domestic Violence, Gio Marconi, Milan

Rien à Signaler, Galerie Analix, Geneva *

Conceptual Living, Rhizome, Amsterdam

1995 Minky Manky, South London Gallery, London

Kwangju Biennale, Korea

Brilliant! New Art from London, Walker Art Center, Minneapolis *

Self Made, Grazer Kunstverein, Graz

Passions Privees, Musee d'Art Moderne, Paris

1996 Do-it, Kjarvalsstadir, Reykjavik

The Cauldron, The Henry Moore Studio, Dean Clough, Halifax *

* Denotes accompanying publication

GEORGINA STARR

born 1968, Leeds

Education

1987–89 Middlesex Polytechnic
1990–92 Slade School of Art

Awards

1992　British Institute Award for Sculpture
　　　Duveen Travel Award
1993–94 Rijksakademie Van Beeldende Kunst,
　　　Amsterdam
1993　VSB Award
　　　Leverhulme Trust Award
　　　Uriot Prize

Solo Exhibitions

1992　Mentioning, Anthony Reynolds Gallery,
　　　London
1994　Getting to Know You, Anthony Reynolds
　　　Gallery, London
　　　(Un)Controlling, Stedelijk Museum
　　　Bureau, Amsterdam
　　　The Nine Collections of the Seventh
　　　Museum, Stroom, Den Haag
　　　Crying, Galerie Krinzinger, Vienna
1995　Visit to a Small Planet, Kunthalle, Zurich
　　　Rooseum, Centre for Contemporary Art,
　　　Malmö
　　　The Party, Bloom Gallery, Amsterdam
　　　(with Alise Tak)
1996　Hypnodreamdruff, Art Now, Tate Gallery,
　　　London
　　　Barbara Gladstone Gallery, New York

Group Exhibitions

1990　Mall Galleries, London
　　　AVE 90, Gemeente Museum, Arnhem
1991　AVE 91, Filmuis, Arnhem
1992　PG6, Slade Gallery, London
　　　Through View, Diorama Gallery, London
1993　Barclays Young Artists, Serpentine
　　　Gallery, London ★
　　　Aperto, Venice Biennale ★
　　　Ha-Ha, Killerton House, Devon ★
　　　Wonderful Life, Lisson Gallery, London ★
　　　Restaurant, La Bocca, Paris
　　　high fidelity, Kohji Ogura Gallery,
　　　Nagoya ★
　　　Open Atellerdagen, Rijksakademie,
　　　Amsterdam
1994　high fidelity, The Rontgen Kunst
　　　Institute, Tokyo

Andrea Rosen Gallery, New York
Looking at Words: Reading Pictures,
Elms Lester, London and touring
Without Walls, The Face magazine
WM Karaoke, Portikus, Frankfurt
Europa 94, Munich
Untitled Streamer Eddy Monkey Full Stop
Etcetera, Anthony Reynolds
Gallery, London
Le Shuttle, Kunstlerhaus Bethanien, Berlin ★
Schipper & Krome, Cologne
Electric Ladyland, Jousse Seguin, Paris
Points de vue (Images d'Europe), Centre
Georges Pompidou, Paris
Use Your Allusion; Recent Video Art,
Museum of Contemporary Art, Chicago
It's how you play the game, Exit Art, New
York
1995　Kunstforeningen, Copenhagen
Anthony Reynolds Gallery, London
Hopeless, Centre for Contemporary Art,
Glasgow
In Search of the Miraculous, Starkmann
Ltd, London
Everytime I See You, Malmö, (Nicolai
Wallner)
La Valise du Celibataire, Maastricht
Couldn't get ahead, IAS, London
Auto Reverse, Saint Gervais, Geneva
Campo, Venice Biennale ★
Here and Now, Serpentine Gallery, London
Wild Walls, Stedelijk Museum,
Amsterdam ★
Ateliers d'Artistes de la Ville de
Marseilles, Marseilles
Night and Day, Anthony Reynolds
Gallery, London
Brilliant! New Art from London, Walker
Art Center, Minneapolis ★
Brill, Montgomerie Galsoe Fine Art,
Minneapolis
Troisième Biennale de Lyon, Lyon
The British Art Show 4, Manchester,
Edinburgh and Cardiff ★
1996　No 10, Rhona Hoffman Gallery, Chicago
Galerie Froment-Putman, Paris
Kunstmuseum Wolfsburg, Wolfsburg
The Cauldron, The Henry Moore Studio,
Dean Clough, Halifax ★

★ Denotes accompanying publication

GILLIAN WEARING

born 1963, Birmingham

Education

1985–87 B TECH Art and Design, Chelsea School
of Art, London

1987–90 BA (Hons) Fine Art, Goldsmiths' College,
London

Awards

1993–94 BT Young Contemporaries

Solo Exhibitions

1993 City Racing, London

1994 Interim Art, London

1995 Western Security, Hayward Gallery,
London

1996 Gillian Wearing, City Projects – Prague,
Part II, The British Council, Prague
Valentina Moncada, Rome (British
Council) ⋆
Interim Art, London

Group Exhibitions

1991 Empty Gestures, Diorama Art Centre,
London
Clove I, The Clove Building, London
Piece Talks, Diorama Art Centre, London

1992 British Art Group Show, Le Musée des
Beaux Arts dans le Havre
Instruction, Marconi Gallery, Milan

1993 Vox Pop, Laure Genillard Gallery,
London
2 into 1, Centre 181 Gallery, London
Mandy Loves Declan 100%, Mark Boote
Gallery, New York
Okay Behaviour, 303 Gallery, New York
BT Young Contemporaries, Cornerhouse,
Manchester and tour

1994 Not Self Portrait, Karsten Schubert
Gallery, London
Rien à Signaler, Gallerie Analix, Geneva ⋆
Domestic Violence, Gio Marconi, Milan
Fouri Fase, Via Farini, Milan
Uncertain Identity, Galerie Analix,
Geneva
3.016.026, Theoretical Events, Naples
Le Shuttle, Kunstlerhaus Bethanien,
Berlin

1995 Pandaemonium: London Festival of
Moving Images, ICA, London
X/Y, Centre Georges Pompidou, Paris

Campo, Venice Biennale ⋆
Sage, Michel Rien, Tours
It's not a picture, Galleria Emi Fontana,
Milan
Brilliant! New Art from London, Walker
Art Center, Minneapolis ⋆
Mysterium Alltag, Kampnagel, Hamburg,
with Jane and Louise Wilson
Tacita Dean, Tracey Emin
Aperto '95, Nouveau Musée, Institut d'Art
Contemporain, Villeurbanne
Hotel Mama (Aperto '95), Kunstraum,
Vienna
Make Believe, Royal College of Art,
London
Mobius Strip, Basilico Fine Arts, New
York
Hello!, Andréhn-Schiptjenko, Stockholm
Gone, Blum & Poe, Los Angeles
The British Art Show 4, Manchester,
Edinburgh and Cardiff ⋆

1996 Private View, The Bowes Museum,
Barnard Castle, County Durham ⋆
NowHere, Louisiana Museum of Modern
Art, Humlebaek, Denmark ⋆
Imagined Communities, Oldham Art
Gallery; John Hansard Gallery,
Southampton; First Colchester; Walsall
Museum & Art Gallery; Royal Festival
Hall, London & Gallery of Modern Art,
Glasgow
The Cauldron, The Henry Moore Studio,
Dean Clough, Halifax ⋆

⋆ Denotes accompanying publication

ILLUSTRATIONS

Christine Borland

p 20
Artificial Wounds and Sores, 5 Bleeding
(detail)
1995
Plastic training injuries, artificial blood
Dimensions vary
Courtesy the artist
Photo Sulyok Mikos

p 21
Underpass (detail)
1995
6 photos, each 25.5 × 25.5 cm
From the series The Velocity of Drops
Courtesy Sean Kelly, New York, and the artist
Photo David Allen

p 22
From Life, Berlin (detail)
1996
21 glass shelves, dust, 21 industrial lamps
Dimensions variable
Kunst-Werke, Berlin
Courtesy the artist
Photo Uwe Walter

p 23
Inside Pocket
1995
8 coats & jackets with altered inside pockets,
8 guns, text
Dimensions variable
British Council Window Gallery, Prague
Courtesy the artist
Photo Martin Polak

p 23
Inside Pocket (detail)
1995
British Council Window Gallery, Prague
Courtesy the artist
Photo Martin Polack

The Cauldron

p 24
2nd Class Male, 2nd Class Female (detail)
1996
Plaster, bronze, text on paper, skulls, cardboard
boxes, polystyrene chips
Dimensions variable

p 25
2nd Class Male, 2nd Class Female (detail)

1996
Plaster, bronze, text on paper, skulls, cardboard
boxes, polystyrene chips
Dimensions variable

All works in The Cauldron courtesy the artist and
the Henry Moore Institute
Installation photos Susan Crowe

Angela Bulloch

p 26
Round Table with Mae West
1995
Arne Jacobsen table, chairs, ice bucket, water jug
and glasses with cushion-activated sound of Mae
West*isms*, photos of Mae West and postcards/Arne
Jacobsen

p 27
Panorama Island
1995
Renamed island in the Thames – work in progress
Commissioned by PADT London
Photo Stephen White

p 28
Betaville
1994
Bench activated drawing machine
Drawing 275 cm square
Photo Fredrik Nilsen

p 29
**Betaville, Happy Sack with Notebooks,
8 Raptures with Remoconboy, Random Reminder**
1995
Photo Fredrik Nilsen

All the above courtesy the artist, PADT, London
and Schipper & Krome, Cologne

The Cauldron

p 30
R360
1996
Vinyl silk paint
800 × 190 cm

p 31
**Grand Stand and the Marxist Myth (A Light
Lowered, A Floor Raised, A Sound Bounced)**
1996
Mixed media
Dimensions variable

Remocon Bags with Grand Stand
1994/1996
2 Remocon Bags: red cotton, diameter 200 cm,
Grand Stand TV game

All works in The Cauldron courtesy the artist and
the Henry Moore Institute
Installation photos Susan Crowe

Dinos & Jake Chapman

p 32
Great Deeds Against the Dead
1994
Mixed media
277 × 244 × 152.5 cm
Photo Sue Omerod

p 33
We are Artists
1992
Mud text installation at Hales Gallery, London
874 × 244 cm
Photo Paul Cousins

p 34
**Zygotic acceleration, biogenetic, de-sublimated
libidinal model (enlarged x 1000)**
1995
Fibreglass, resin, paint
180 × 150 × 140 cm

p 35
Übermensch (detail)
1995
Fibreglass, resin, paint
Height c. 365 cm

All the above courtesy the Victoria Miro Gallery,
London

The Cauldron

p 36
Gold, Silver & Shit
1996
Painted gold, silver and shit
3 works, each 10 × 10 cm on 300 × 300 cm table

p 37
Gold, Silver & Shit
1996
Painted gold, silver and shit
3 works, each 10 × 10 cm on 300 × 300 cm table

All works in The Cauldron courtesy the artist and
the Henry Moore Institute
Installation photos Susan Crowe

Steven Pippin

p 38
Negative Perspective
1995
Photograph on board
610 × 457 cm
Courtesy the artist
Photo M. Michalski & B. Wojcik

p 39
Cosmos (detail)
1995
Aluminium, perspex, rubber, record player, motor,
loudspeaker, vinyl recording of Einstein, vacuum
106 × 124 × 56 cm
Courtesy the artist
Photo the artist

p 40
Stereophonic Wow & Flutter
1994
Aluminium, motor, amplifier, stylus, loudspeakers,
2 × single loops of recorded sound on vinyl
133 × 41 × 28 cm
Courtesy the artist and the Victoria Miro Gallery,
London
Photo the artist

The Cauldron

p 41
Horizontal Hold
1996
(Shown in the artist's studio)
Aluminium, television set, video transmitter,
video player
Height 122 × diameter 127 cm
Photo the artist

p 41
Horizontal Hold
1996
Sketch on paper
25 × 17.7 cm
Courtesy the artist

p 42
Horizontal Hold
1996
Aluminium, television set, video transmitter,
video player
Height 122 × diameter 127 cm

p 43
Horizontal Hold
1996
Aluminium, television set, video transmitter,
video player
Height 122 × diameter 127 cm

All works in The Cauldron courtesy the artist and
the Henry Moore Institute
Installation photos Susan Crowe

Georgina Starr

p 44
The Nine Collections of the Seventh Museum
1994
Installation view
Mixed media
Dimensions vary

p 45
Crying
1993
Video
Duration 4 min

p 46
The Party, Entertaining the Guests
1995
Video
Duration 25 min

p 47
**Hypnodreamdruff: The Hungry Brain, Elena
singing Schizophrenia** (detail)
1996
Installation
Mixed media

All the above courtesy Anthony Reynolds Gallery,
London

The Cauldron

p 48
Drivin On
1996
Painted wooden car 350 × 150 cm, video
Duration 6 min

p 49
Drivin On (detail)
1996
Video

All works in The Cauldron courtesy the artist and
the Henry Moore Institute
Installation photos Susan Crowe

Gillian Wearing

p 50
Dancing in Peckham
1994
Video
Duration 25 min

p 51
**Confess all on video. Don't worry you will be in
disguise. Intrigued? Call Gillian…**
1994
Video
Duration 30 min

p 51
**Confess all on video. Don't worry you will be in
disguise. Intrigued? Call Gillian…**
1994
Video
Duration 30 min

p 52
**Signs that say what you want them to say and
not signs that say what someone else wants you
to say**
1992–93
C-print mounted on aluminium
30 × 17 × 1 cm

p 53
**Homage to the woman with the bandaged face
who I saw yesterday down Walworth Road**
1995
Video
Duration 7 min

All the above courtesy Interim Art, London

The Cauldron

p 54
60 Minutes Silence
1996
Video back-projection
Duration 60 min

p 55
60 Minutes Silence
1996
Video back-projection
Duration 60 min

All works in The Cauldron courtesy the artist and
the Henry Moore Institute
Installation photos Susan Crowe

NOTES

1. *Gilbert & George*, 1984, published by Baltimore (The Baltimore Museum Of Art), page 15, catalogue essay by Brenda Richardson. 'We want to *un-shock* people and bringing these subjects into the open, allowing them to live and breath, should un-shock', Gilbert and George.

2. Julie Burchill's article *The Fine Art Of Being A New Fascist* appeared in *The Sunday Times*, 1st October 1995. '...(The Chapmans) are, they claim proudly, "sadistic and anal". Well, so was Hitler, and I don't recall the civil liberties lobby speaking up for *him...*' Much of Burchill's comments misquote Dinos and Jake Chapman from an earlier article entitled 'Dedicated Followers Of Fascism' in *The Observer Review* 1995 written by Charlotte O'Sullivan.

3. Charles Esche, page 7, catalogue entitled *Christine Borland*, published by Tramway, November 1994, to coincide with the exhibition *From Life* – a Tramway/Kunst-Werke collaboration.

4. Steven Pippin, pages 6–7, *The Rigmarole Of Photography*, published on the occasion of the exhibition, *Introspective*, held at the ICA, London, 1993.

5. 'The future of photography seems to rely on the progress of the camera and its ability to be continually refined, to a point whereby images will be indistinguishable from reality. Working in the opposite direction to this mentality I have become fascinated with the idea of constructing a camera whose viewpoint is not some external subject, but instead one having the capability of looking back in on itself towards its own darkness.' Steven Pippin, pages 6–7, *The Rigmarole Of Photography*, published on the occasion of the exhibition, *Introspective*, held at the ICA, London, 1993.

6. *Wild Walls*, Stedelijk Museum Amsterdam. Artists: Kai Althoff, John Currin, Douglas Gordon, Gary Hume, Multiple Autorenschaft Lienz, Lara Schnitger, Georgina Starr, Mat Collishaw, Anne Decock, Benoît Hermans, Arnout Mik, Pipilotti Rist, Manfre Du Schu, Jane & Louise Wilson. 15 September – 29 October 1995.

7. Georgina Starr interviewed by Adam Chodzko, page 39, *Tate, The Art Magazine*. Spring Issue 1996.

8. Refer to *Discovering the Secrets of... Steven Pippin*, British Council/FRAC Limousin, page 98, portrait photograph entitled *Pippin, Flamstead House, Greenwich, 23 mars 1995*.

Published on the occasion
of the exhibition

The Cauldron

at the Henry Moore Studio
Dean Clough, Halifax

31 May – 4 August 1996

An exhibition organised by
the Henry Moore Institute and
selected by Maureen Paley

Sponsored by

Published by
The Henry Moore Sculpture Trust
The Henry Moore Institute
74 The Headrow, Leeds LS1 3AA

© The author, the artists and
the Henry Moore Institute

ISBN 1 900081 65 2

Photos of The Henry Moore Studio
pages 2 and 71 Susan Crowe

Studio photographs
pages 4–17 Gregor Muir

Design/production
Groundwork, Skipton

Printed in Great Britain

HENRY MOORE
INSTITUTE